Energize Your Entrepreneurial Spirit

52 TIPS TO GET YOU STARTED ON YOUR PATH TO SUCCESS

Scott Ward
Jeff Ward
with Andréa Ledding

Energize Your Entrepreneurial Spirit

52 TIPS TO GET YOU STARTED ON YOUR PATH TO SUCCESS

Suite 425, 800 Kelly Rd.
Victoria, BC V9B 6J9

To order additional copies or to book Jeff & Scott for speaking engagements please call the booking office at 1-877-347-0663.

June 2011 Edition
ISBN 978-0-9877091-0-3
Printed in Canada by Island Blue

Cover photo by Troy Moth
Book layout & design by Jeff Ward
Additional editing by Dewayne Ward

We thank our friends, family & community for their support and encouragement.

Special thanks to Andréa Ledding for helping us take our thoughts into book form :)

Additional thanks to our Uncle Bruce Barry for helping us get this project off the ground.

Table Of Contents

"Success is not a doorway, it's a staircase."
—Dottie Walters

The Successful Mindset

The number one thing you need to succeed in business is a successful attitude. A successful attitude means accepting that everyone's life is not fair, but that everyone can still succeed if they take responsibility for themselves and their own actions, and don't expect to be handed everything on a silver platter. You may have encountered all kinds of difficulties in your life, but you are not unique. Each of us as human beings need to struggle in order to grow, and luckily struggles are something that are impossible to avoid. Begin to look at your experiences and the difficulties in your life as gifts that have made you the strong, resilient, unique person that you are. Recognize that perseverance, wisdom and creativity result from overcoming obstacles, not avoiding them, or living a life free from difficulty, pain, or failure.

Failure is an important part of life, and handling failure successfully greatly contributes to making a person successful. We all experience failure. As the saying goes, "suck it up, buttercup" — learn the lesson and use the experience to grow wiser, not angrier, more bitter or discouraged. Expecting to live a life without mistakes is not only unreasonable, it's boring. Mistakes are one way we, as human beings, learn and grow. Every mistake made is a teachable moment, a moment to learn what you are made of and what actions don't work so they aren't repeated.

The wisest learners, however, will learn not only from their own successes, mistakes and failures, but from those of others. This is why we are writing this book: to share what we have learned along the way. We want to let you know that while you aren't the first or the last to make mistakes, if you give yourself permission to be a lifelong learner and permission to fail, you will eventually succeed. Guaranteed. So read on. And when you fail, dust yourself off, regroup - and get back up on the horse.

Scott Says: *There were times that I felt like throwing in the towel, but with self-employment you can change directions and proceed a different way when you need to.*

"To find out what one is fitted to do, and to secure an opportunity to do it, is the key to happiness." —**John Dewey**

What Are Your Gifts?

Recognizing and writing down your gifts is as important, if not more important, than writing down your goals. Writing down your goals is a useful tool to work concretely towards achieving your dreams and visions. Recognizing your gifts and callings is what creates those dreams and visions in the first place, and nurtures a positive and strength-based attitude.

Successful individuals focus on their gifts and strengths, not their weaknesses or flaws. Everyone has his or her areas of strength. Successful people learn to use their assets to their advantage, and realistically minimize or work around their deficits.

Every human being is born with varying degrees of potential – but all of us also have natural talents and abilities that, over time, become unique to us depending on our latent ability, our environment, our personality, our experiences, and all the millions of influences that affect human beings. Everyone is good at something, and there is no one who is not good at anything! So we need to focus on those unique positives, and try to work in our areas of personal gifting: music, art, baking, sports, carpentry, cooking, cleaning, listening skills, public speaking, teaching, leadership – the list could go on forever. Allow what is good in you to get out and work for you.

Once you have made a list of your gifts – and feel free to ask others who know you well what they think your special gifts are – take a look at the list. Of the many gifts, what are you really passionate about? What stands out as something you really love doing that connects with you?

Once you have narrowed it down, start thinking of how to direct your gifts and passion. Filling a need in your community, or the community beyond, with the particular set of gifts that you've been given, the passion to pursue them and taking action to make your dreams come true: that is where you will find success.

Individual gifts + personal passion + action = success for everyone.

Jeff Says: *I'm all for learning new things, however, if there is something that you're already good at you'll see more return on investment if you perfect your craft rather than focusing on things that don't come easily to you.*

"We make a living by what we get, but we make a life by what we give." —**Winston Churchill**

You Don't Need Other People's Money To Start A Business

It's easy to fall into the trap of thinking you need start-up money for a business, and the only way to get that is through other people (because you don't have a big pile of money sitting around waiting to be spent, do you? If you do, what are you waiting for – go start your business!)

There are three problems with borrowing other people's money. First of all, most other people don't have a big pile of money sitting around waiting to be spent either (and if they do, there is probably a big lineup for their money pile!) Not everyone or every business idea qualifies for a bank loan.

Secondly, if you take other people's money, you generally have to do what they want you to do – and that is the opposite of working for yourself. It's a lot easier to be your own boss when you don't already have one. If you lose money along the way, it's a lot easier to lose your own money than money borrowed from someone else — whether you have to deal with hard feelings, disappointed family members, or worse!

Thirdly, having to pay back loans from elsewhere will seriously hurt your cash flow in a fledgling business.

So, if you don't have the necessary cash to get started, why not earn it? You'll appreciate it more. You will gain valuable experience along the way. Start a service business – find a need you can fill, find out how much you can charge, keep your costs and overhead low, and away you go. It can also be as simple as taking a second job, or merely disciplining yourself to save by setting aside as much as you can with every cheque.

The important thing is to find a project, earn the money you need, and re-invest in what you're really passionate about. It's only going to fuel your dreams and your drive to succeed if you've worked and saved your way towards that goal. Invest in yourself.

Scott Says: *My first real business was shoveling my elderly neighbour's sidewalk. I provided a service because she was a senior citizen and she always paid me after I was done. This was my first job but I didn't realize it was a business till I was much older!*

"Just do it." —**Nike**

The Hardest Part Is Starting

When you're running a race, everyone lines up at the starting line, poised and ready. The signal is given – a starter's pistol – adrenaline pumping, the runners take off. This isn't quite the same way we start off our personal projects, unless we're becoming world-class athletes. Even world class athletes do a lot more work on their own the other 364 days of the year, compared to those few seconds spent on the track trying to win gold.

So where do you start? Well, just as you listed your gifts, start with a list of what you need to do – from the smallest detail to the largest thing you can think of that needs to happen to get your plan off the ground. Don't worry about any particular order at first, just write it down or type it out as it comes to you, for as long as it takes. When you're done the list, congratulate yourself – the hardest part of anything is getting started, and you just got started, one item at a time.

But, making a list isn't the same as actually accomplishing the things on your list, so don't get too self-congratulatory – you still have some work ahead of you. It can be overwhelming looking at a seemingly never-ending to-do list. The only way to deal with that sense of feeling defeated before you even get going, is to start with the first task that looks the most fun or the easiest for you to accomplish – what an orchard worker would call "low hanging fruit." Go for the easy mark first, and get that rewarding sense of accomplishment that comes with checking something off the list, because that sense of accomplishment will get you into the zone of building on your success and you'll gain momentum towards completing more and more of the tasks you have before you.

By the time you get to the end of the list, you'll have accomplished so much, and you'll be feeling so good about yourself that those things that looked so hard will be easy to check off. Use this trick every time you feel overwhelmed: it's a tool to help you succeed.

Jeff Says: *When I get overwhelmed with a long to-do list and I feel like procrastinating, I trick myself into only doing one task and one task only. As soon as I know it, I'm "in the zone", that procrastination bug is squashed and I'm getting things done.*

"Any path is only a path and there is no affront to oneself or to others, in dropping it if that is what your heart tells you."
—Carlos Castaneda

From "Hobby" To "Business"

Hobbies are those interests we pursue, and those passions we find along life's path. Sometimes it's a lifelong interest. Other times, it's something we stumble across and begin to explore or develop, or something a friend or acquaintance introduces to us. But what happens when breeding goldfish suddenly becomes more than a hobby, when you become known as a source of quality goldfish for other goldfish aficionados? Then you've reached that point in the road where hobby meets business.

When you are able to make money while doing your hobby — something you love, are interested in, have expertise in — it's a good indication that maybe you've found yourself a business.

What are some things you should consider first? Is it a good idea to turn every hobby into a business? What if you love building furniture, and people say they're willing to pay you to do it, but you think you might get sick of it if it becomes mere work, a day to day job? The key is to carefully consider doing this as full-time business. If you think you won't get sick of your hobby, then go for it. What have you got to lose? You have demonstrated you have individual gifts and personal passion to build furniture and now just need to turn this into a business.

So what are some things to look for in a situation like this? Firstly, a hobby-turned-business should, at the very least, pay for itself. If you are selling paintings, you want to make enough not only to pay for your supplies used, but also to buy more (and paying for the time and labour you put in is also nice.) Some paintings are worth more than others because of the talent, skill, and time invested, not just the material or subject matter. So keep that in mind when creating your payscale, and be realistic. For example, paying someone else to do the preparation of the canvas, has to be worth the time of both parties. It might be that part of your business can and should be contracted out to others. This way you can focus on what you most enjoy that which requires your gifts and skills. But, remember, you must also be willing and able to pay your co-hobbyists what their work is worth and still manage to make a profit.

Scott Says: *When I first ventured out as a stage hypnotist I was willing to perform for free. After I started getting requests to perform, very quickly I had to make a choice about charging a fee for service.*

"But I can't keep runnin' I just gotta keep keen and cunnin'."
—Pharcyde

Decide If Travelling Is Worth It To You

Travelling is a great way to expand your business, make those face-to-face contacts, network with others, and see interesting new places while you work. But there are some downsides and important considerations. When your business potentially involves travel, the first thing you need to decide is: does your health, family, and home life support it? No business is worth sacrificing any of these three items. Do you get so sick on airplanes or rough highways that it takes too much out of you? Do you have young children with separation anxiety? Do you provide care for an elder, or are you a single parent who needs to work close to home?

If the answer appears to be 'yes' to those aspects of travel, then you need to decide how much time you are willing to sacrifice — whether that time is spent flying across the country, driving to the next town, or dog sledding to remote areas. A wise use of your time is crucial in every business. While each business is unique, if you are away too long from your home base, it can get tricky to stay on top of things and still effectively grow your business.

Another important consideration is cost: can you and your business afford the expense? Good planning and budgeting of both time and money for each trip will help you build your business, as well as seeing more of the world around you.

Here's something to consider if you do have family waiting eagerly for your return: always bring something back for your loved ones, especially the kids. Our Dad always did, even if it was as simple as a free bag of peanuts from the airplane, and it's a tradition we've continued.

Jeff Says: *When I travel, I try to find opportunities to bring my family with me. Kids love hotels with swimming pools!*

"Long-term planning is not about making decisions, it is about understanding the future consequences of today's decisions."
—Gary Ryan Blair

Once You Get "The Big Idea" Don't Give It Up!

So you have a gift, a passion, and vision for your business. Maybe you've worked out some of the details, maybe there are obstacles in the way, or in your mind, you're not making enough money. Maybe you're making so much money you think it's time to go while the getting is good. Whatever the case: now is not the time to throw in the towel — you're just getting started.

It's important to realize that you're in this for the long haul. You are not here to make a quick buck and leave town on the midnight train. Besides, that kind of mentality encourages shady business practices and can give you a bad reputation. Why would you put all that labour, love, and effort into birthing a business, and then sell it off like a day-old donut? You need to think of your business as a long-term investment, even as a long-term relationship if you don't mind the comparison. You have put time, effort, money and love into this relationship, and there is a payoff — your business is going to provide for you and yours. You need to do what it takes to be focused, excited, and committed to your business and your dreams. Stay your course.

Another thing to keep in mind is that just because you have a big idea doesn't mean you're the only one who had, or will have, it. There will be others who will have the same idea — or perhaps be inspired when they see you in action — but that is no reason to get discouraged. In fact, you should see it as evidence that your idea was a good one, if you have others trying to copy you. Remember the saying that imitation is the sincerest form of flattery, that there is room for everyone at the table. Focus on bringing out the best in yourself and sharing your unique offerings with others.

Scott Says: *I told myself the next big idea that I got, I would action it and work until it came to fruition.*

"Yesterday is history, tomorrow is a mystery, today is a gift. That's why we call it 'the present'."
—Unknown

Get Excited For Monday Morning!

Are you one of those people who dread the beginning of the work week? One way to modify your negative thinking about Monday morning is to focus on all the opportunities it brings to move you closer to a better life. That is the reality of what Monday morning offers you. It will help you become excited about what opportunities you have right in front of you, as opposed to stressing about what you believe you don't have.

Your team takes your lead, so you start by simply making a decision to think differently, deciding that you are going to be happy and excited to go to work. We are not talking about 'fake it until you make it', but rather about you opting to take control of your thoughts, and how you are going to emotionally respond to the world. Note, we stated 'respond' to the world, not 'react' – they are different things. A reaction is 'action without control' and response is 'action under control': a position of strength.

Why don't you feel excited about going to work? In our experience, most people give too much power to the unknown, believing the abyss is much deeper than it is. The very first step you need to take on this journey is to accept that you are in control of your emotions. Emotions are not involuntary or random. This fact is often lost amongst the habitual fear, negativity, anxiety and distress of our modern world. Yet, once you realize that you are, in fact, the 'boss of you', there is a major shift in your outlook on life.

Set new challenges for yourself at work, small ones, big ones, but most importantly 'new' ones. Keep track of them so you can look back when you need encouragement. This is one way to shake up the day-in/day-out routine, plus providing measurable success. Likewise, it will make you more attentive and motivated when you have a goal.

Scott Says: *Once I found my calling to self-employment I became excited to get up Mondays because I was able to action my ideas that were brewing all weekend, and Monday is the best day to make decisions for the week.*

"Work and play are words used to describe the same thing under differing conditions."
—Mark Twain

Don't Do It If You Don't Love It!

For a lot of people work is a mind-numbing, body-sucking drain of time and energy that is scarcely tolerated so that hopefully, one day, a few minutes of joy can be purchased before returning 'back to the grindstone'. Why? Frequently the cause is a misplaced belief that life is some kind of horribly bitter cough medicine, which, only if endured frequently and regularly, becomes 'good for you'. We believe that there is no redoing this life, that humans were not created for endless misery. This existence is not a dry run for the next, so please stop wasting your time.

Every moment you waste putting off doing something you love is time you will never get back. Don't spend countless days stressed and bored completing repetitive tasks. Doing something you love is life-changing for you and everyone you meet. Change one person (you!) and change the world forever.

'Do what you love' is not a new idea. We've all heard this before, but what people miss is that every second of delay becomes a minute, an hour, a day, and a lifetime. There is urgency, so start doing something now — in this next moment — that you love. Take a piece of paper 'now', and write down what you would really like to be doing. Use it as a bookmark while you continue reading this book. Now put the book down, and don't come back until you've done something you love. Remember, someone really important is watching your every move — you. So no cheating. Go do something you love, something you've been putting off for far too long.

And remember to dream big: you deserve it!

Jeff Says: *If I'm not absolutely passionate about what I do everyday then I'm going to change what I do to something else that I am passionate about.*

"Courage is the mastery of fear, not the absence of fear.." **—Mark Twain**

When To Leave The Day Job

Suppose you've been in the service industry, or mid-career in a job you can't stand, or you're simply putting in time ensuring you have the capital to fund your real passion. How do you know when to make the full transition? The most important thing is to have a plan: if you were planning for a vacation, you'd have a budget, a timeline, an idea of your basic costs and overhead and necessary savings/potential earnings. Well, now you're planning for the vacation of a lifetime — so follow the same basic format. Map it out and follow it.

A good rule to follow is: once you are earning as much as your full-time job, (or you are well on track to doing so, once you have the full-time opportunity to dedicate to it), and especially if you are running out of evening or weekend hours, that is the time to stop rowing two boats.

While you're building your business and waiting to achieve a full-time transition, find out what your options are with your current employer. Can you take gradual leave, work part-time, or take temporary time off just to be sure? The transition is going to largely depend on what kind of job you're leaving behind. If it's a fantastic government job with plenty of benefits, holidays and a huge salary, you may want to look into those benefits and see if you can take some kind of year-long sabbatical to explore your business options. This means you still have a safety net, and a guaranteed way to return if things don't quite pan out the way you'd planned. On the other hand, if you're in the kind of job that just requires sufficient notice for your boss to replace you with another warm body, make that phone call or write that formal resignation letter after you've carefully outlined your transition plans. It's not like you can't find another job (or return to the same one) if you really need to.

Try to leave on good terms, of course. You will want to keep as much goodwill as you can because you own a business now and word of mouth and reputation are important! Your old employers or co-workers may become your most eager customers or promoters.

Scott Says: *Knowing when to leave my fulltime employment was one of the most difficult decisions I had to make. You need to make a plan for it — just like one would make a plan to take a trip to Hawaii. You need to start planning a date to leave your day job and how you will do it!*

"In truth, people can generally make time for what they choose to do; it is not really the time but the will that is lacking."
—Sir John Lubbock

Put More Time Into Your Business Than You Did Working As An Employee

You're on the hook now — boss, employee, and business owner all in one. This is not time to kick back and relax. You need to put the same amount of working hours into your new job as you did with your old one, probably even more. After all, who is more motivated about your own business than you are? So, if you've left your old job and you're expecting to make a go of it, doesn't it make sense to put, at a minimum, the same amount of time and effort into this business as you did at your previous job where you were working for someone else?

Not only will you gain from every last hour and every bit of effort invested into your venture, but this business is also yours to lose if you don't give it the necessary time, honour, respect, and commitment that your dreams and passions and gifts deserve. Being your boss means a certain amount of freedom, yes. But with added freedom comes added responsibility (remember the quote from Spiderman, the Movie: "With great power comes great responsibility.")

Use your powers for good — your business deserves to be treated like a business, not a pastime. You are already in the habit of dedicating a certain amount of hours to working for someone else — why wouldn't you keep that habit, but dedicate it towards feeding your own dreams and visions for a successful business model?

Remember: this is your business, your dream, and it is worthwhile. But the success — or failure — is entirely up to just one person. You.

Scott Says: *You WILL be successful if you put in full-time hours working your business. The first three years of your start-up be prepared to put in the hours because there will be a lot of work and you might be your only employee.*

"You gain strength, courage, and confidence by every experience in which you really stop to look fear in the face... the danger lies in refusing to face the fear, in not daring to come to grips with in... you must do the thing you think you cannot do."

—Eleanor Roosevelt

People May Think You Are Crazy When You First Venture Out

Accept that not everyone is going to be as keen about your decision to become an entrepreneur. So what? Make solid decisions, do your homework, set realistic markers to gauge your success, and avoid negativity — much of which is fear based. The only power you have is over you and your reactions, not the words or actions of others. But, if people in your life are toxic, learn to ignore their toxicity or get them out of your life.

Remember, one of the first steps to your success is your own personal commitment to, and confidence in, achieving your goals. In this case, it is all about you.

Like the inevitability of winter, many things are easier to live with once you accept they are going to happen, no matter what. Direct your energy and worry only towards things within your control. Let go of things you have no power over. Accept that some will listen to your news with 'that look,' as if down the road they expect to be reading about you in some medical journal. So what, move on.

This doesn't mean disregard those opinions you trust. Don't be afraid to consider your decision from the position of those who disagree with you. Is there merit to their view, even though it's contrary to your vision? Is there something you haven't thought of yet, or do they have points worth considering? If you are wrong, like all of us at times, it wouldn't be a first. What wins the day is getting up one more time than you've been knocked down. Don't be afraid to consider other points of view. However, don't surrender to unnecessary doubt. We have seen many entrepreneurs with great futures stop short of success, often because they did not surround themselves with quality people and didn't stay the course. A disciplined mind and a positive attitude win the day.

You become the person you want to be and live the life you want for you and your family by being steadfast in your goals. A positive mindset, focusing on the positive, is an important part of your skill set. After all, once you've done market research, gotten a handle on market size, obtained strategic guidance to protect your competitive position, then figured out how you are going to celebrate your success, you really don't have time for negative people, do you?

Scott Says: *I remember when I told my family I was going to quit teaching and my government job to pursue a career 'on stage'. People thought I was crazy.*

"It's faith in something and enthusiasm for something that makes a life worth living."
—Oliver Wendell Holmes

Energy & Enthusiasm

Capital, equipment, service, product, advertising, business plan, and office space — none of these things matter if you don't back them up with your energy and enthusiasm. If you aren't excited about what you're offering, how can you expect your customers to be? Your energy and your enthusiasm are the gas in the engine, so to speak. Without that fuel, you won't get far down the road.

Once again, this is where knowing yourself, and how you work best, comes in handy. What gives you energy? If going for a run every morning helps you do your best thinking and have your best day — make sure you do it. That may be the way you charge up for your day. On the other hand, if being in front of and around people and networking or brainstorming is what fuels you, make sure you plan that into your day too. Every person is uniquely motivated and energized — figure out what works best for you, and use that to your advantage.

Another way to keep your energy and enthusiasm is to make sure you are focusing on the aspects of your business that you absolutely love, those which connect best with your gifts and passions. It's easy to do what you love all day long, however, there are parts of everyone's day or business that still have to get done but aren't in that sweet zone. Granted, some of these little things just have to be muscled through or taken care of — but not always. It's important to keep an eye out for tasks that can be delegated to others. Especially tasks you dislike, tasks that are time-consuming, or tasks that meet more of your weaknesses than your strengths.

Remember: it all has to get done, but that doesn't mean you have to do it all. Your energy and enthusiasm deserve to be protected and saved for what you specialize in. Let someone else who has different specialties use their gifts to shine and help you out at the same time. Energy comes easily when you're working on your passion, and work becomes play when you have enthusiasm. So share the load, and share the joy!

Jeff Says: *There are certain things I'm great at and a few things I'm not. The things I'm not enthusiastic about are inevitably the things that drain my energy. So I find a way to not do them.*

"Sometimes your best investments are the ones you don't make." —**Donald Trump**

If It Won't Pay Off Don't Do It

Everything you do, everything you purchase, and everything you invest in should pay for itself. There are times when your efforts or investments will not pay off immediately — it may be down the road, whether that's tomorrow, next month, or next year. Make sure everything you do counts towards keeping your business in the black (cash in needs to be greater than cash out!) This is an important rule to keep in mind every single time you open your wallet or decide how to spend your business day.

When you're running your own business, expenses can sneak up on you and eat your profit (and then some!) if you don't think in terms of the bottom line at all times. Time-wasting interruptions that don't help your business can erode precious time and energy, stealing from your dreams and business. Be on guard.

Think things through — take that extra few minutes to calculate how much you need to sell to make a certain advertising campaign or piece of equipment pay off. Always look for alternatives: is there a way to accomplish your objective successfully while spending less time, money, and effort? Do you really need to buy the latest/best/coolest/ newest gadget, or is it more efficient to make do with what you have? On the other hand, if you're constantly driving to get something printed out, what would the savings be in terms of time, gas, energy, and actual cost if you purchased a high-end printer, ink, and paper? Don't be afraid to crunch numbers, cost things out, or ask for advice from others. You will have the satisfaction of knowing you are operating as efficiently as possible, and that every investment is worthwhile and paying for itself in some way.

Time and money are both important capital investments and you need to try to maximize both into being used as efficiently as possible.

Jeff Says: *If I buy a new piece of technology I want to make sure that I can put this to use in some sort of way that will make me money down the road. A computer is a good example of this.*

"The key is in not spending time, but in investing it." —**Stephen R. Covey**

Optimize Your Work Time

There are many ways to work at an optimal level, but maximizing your personal work cycle moves you closer to obtaining a life of quality that best suits your individual philosophy and the way you are hard-wired to work most efficiently.

Knowing, or learning, how you work best is the secret to optimizing your work time. Also taking the time to observe and know how, why, when and where you work best, and conversely, when you are not at your prime, is important.

Like everyone, your work cycle will have points of maximum productivity, points of 'near zero' productivity, and points in between. Personal insight and planning around your own 'highs and lows' optimizes your output, gives predictability to your schedule and make your days overall, more satisfying.

Take note when and where you are the most (and least) productive. Don't feel guilty about one part of your work cycle being less productive than another. Every person is like this.

Be aware of personal tendencies and habits regarding the best times of the day for you to be productive. Keep in mind best tasks for certain times, best physical settings and any recurring personal, family and work commitments you have. You also must decide how you are going to deal with unforeseen tasks that come up and have to be dealt with.

It is easier to optimize your work cycle if you work solo as you will not have the unpredictability of office interruptions. If you do have others to consider, try to give yourself 'protected time' during your optimal/peak performance hours.

Jeff Says: *I know I work best for certain tasks from 9 to noon. Even during that time there are other particular tasks better done between 9 a.m. to 11 a.m. But between 2 and 4 in the afternoon, it is time to go for a walk or coffee. I am more productive and likely easier to live with when I follow my personal inclination.*

"Identify your problems, but give your power and energy to solutions." **—Anthony Robbins**

If You Don't Put Energy In, The Clients Will Fade

You need to have a system for success in order to grow and maintain your business. An important part of this is making sure you put in at least enough energy to keep the clients you have, and expand your business at a rate that allows you to take care of each client.

Remember, your clients are the investors in your success. They are number one. Remember the old adage, "the customer is always right," at least when it comes to being given prompt, courteous, quality attention! You need to keep your investors engaged in what you are doing — whether that's through a blog, friendly phone call or coffee to check in, or an emailed quarterly newsletter that lets everyone know what's new. This will depend on your personality, your strengths, and the type of business you're in. But however you decide to do it, DO IT! The personal touch is what can make, or break, a business.

Besides just putting energy into your current clientele, you create further potential clients when you go above and beyond by giving the best product or service. Customer loyalty is earned, but once you have it, word of mouth is the best advertising! Think about it — when a respected friend tells you they have a fantastic, reasonable, reliable, and honest service-provider — don't you pay more attention than when that annoying radio ad with the cheesy jingle is being played for the fourteenth time in a half-hour? Besides, personal referrals are the cheapest and most effective ad campaign you can ask for because it means that simply being awesome to your present clientele will grow you a wider customer base!

So, what's important is to consistently put in the energy to engage your clients, the people who are assisting you in making your dreams come true. Your clients are your business partners, and can be your best resources — never forget it.

Scott Says: *Many times I've seen people fail in their business basically because they didn't put a sustained effort into getting more work. One should never feel too confident during busier times because in a few months these could slow. Start planting client seeds NOW!*

"People who say they sleep like a baby usually don't have one."
—Leo J. Burke

Don't Pull An All-Nighter

Those four words are pretty much explanatory and good common sense as well. We understand how tempting it may be to, "just this once" stay up extremely late or even not go to bed at all, in order to finish off that one project as your deadline looms. If you have ever found yourself in that position, or think you may find yourself in that position, three words, friend: Don't. Do. It.

First of all, your body is designed to sleep on a regular basis. This is when you are supposed to heal, restore, rest, and gain energy, health, and perspective. If you miss sleep, you are robbing your present — because your productivity is going to be shot as the night wears on, and be worse than shot by the next day — and your future, too, because sooner or later that accumulated sleep deficit is going to have to be addressed. Not only will your productivity take an immediate dive and your general mental and emotional state be less even-keeled, but your body's ability to ward things off — your immune system — will be more vulnerable. You can end up going further backwards than forwards; you will pay, your family and friends will pay, your clients will pay and ultimately your business will feel the negative effects. It's just not worth it, no matter how you look at it!

Secondly, this is just a bad space to be in — if you are at a point where you are working 24 hours a day, something is wrong and unbalanced in your life and it's time to take a good hard look at what that may be. Are you taking on too much? Not making effective use of your time? Leaving too much until the last minute? Failing to delegate those things you are not strong at? Working with substandard tools or a disorganized workspace? Whatever is causing you to get to this point where you can't even get to bed, analyze and isolate it and then figure out a solution.

People who are trying to work 24 hours a day in order to look good usually end up looking bad. People who burn out trying to impress others are never fooling anyone. Except themselves. You deserve to get a decent night's sleep just like every other person in this world. So don't fall into this trap — none of us are robots, everyone needs sleep. Even you.

Jeff Says: *Dealing with teething babies or sick kids through the night can be tiring enough but on top of that add an evening up late working. That's a recipe for disaster.*

"Home is where the heart is."
— Pliny the Elder

Home Based Office

Having a successful office in your home can save money, provide a tax advantage, and improve both you and your family's quality of life. But there are also things to look out for, and with experience, we have discovered how to deal with the challenges of a home office. With some thought and planning to your specific situation, you can maximize your productivity and make it all work.

Even when we had offices away from home, we both had to deal with thoughts and distractions around family issues. Granted, having an office in our homes has not done away with this, but the distractions are welcome and we're grateful we get to spend more time each day with our families, including the saved drive time of the commute. Of course there are always 'little bugs' to work out. It's called 'living life.' Here are some tips.

If you can afford two phones, have one in your 'work office space' and the other in the family area. Fight the temptation to have two lines on the same phone set. Why? No doubt you have this scene in your mind where you quickly answer the 'business line' while making lunch in the kitchen. This is a slippery slope that will obstruct your ability to concentrate on business and also teaches family that your workspace is open to them as part of the family space. After all, if you can come into their space and 'do business', why do they need to respect your business space?

'Working space' and 'family space' ought to be, and are, different and separate things. You need the family space to relax in. Be mindful, as the distinction can all too easily slip away.

Establish and keep business hours. You need to know when you are working, your family needs to know when you are working, and most importantly, your clients and customers need to know when you are working. Also allow for, and honour, break times.

Get a mailbox outside of your home. This will give you a secure address for business, protect your home address and, again, separate business from home. If you think it'll work in your situation, there are many reasons to have an office in your home.

Jeff Says: *I've got a sweet home office setup that is away from the family common areas, which enables me to be out of sight during the day. I have an open-door policy with my kids but if I close my door they know I'm on the phone or can't be disturbed so they know to knock… quietly.*

"Don't work for money. Make money work for you." – **Robert T. Kiyosaki**

Work Smart, Not Hard

While you need to put a certain amount of time and energy into your business, you also need a balanced approach. Working 14 hour days, 7 days a week, is neither fun, nor sustainable. And it is not why you got into business for yourself, is it? If this is the way you are working, you need to take a hard look at why. Are there things in your life you are trying to avoid by over-working? Start dealing with them. While every person needs to have meaningful work in their lives, escaping their lives completely by immersing themselves in work means, well ... 'no life at all.' So, get a life! Whatever that means to you: rebuilding relationships, making new friends, reconnecting with old friends, spending time with your family, volunteering, or making the time for another endeavour you've always meant to.

If you're working long hours simply because you're falling behind, again take a look at why and find a solution. Don't keep running at the brick wall full-tilt. Stop and ask yourself what is going wrong. Maybe you need to start delegating more, or look at hiring out some parts of the work which are especially time-consuming, challenging, or simply not enjoyable. Money is time, and time is money, so don't forget to put your money to work by buying your time back. It's about finding a balance. Nowhere is it written that just because you are self-employed you need to do everything everywhere for everyone!

Another way your money can work for you is by investing it. If you have some savings, look at making wise investments which return money to you on a regular basis. Once you have money, learn to use it as a tool to buy back your time or have it earn its own keep with interest or investment payoffs. Remember, part of the reason you started working for yourself was the freedom it offered — not a new slavery! So, practice efficiency and remember to take enough time off on a daily, weekly, monthly, and annual basis, so that you remain productive, enthusiastic, focused, and balanced.

Jeff Says: *I hired a virtual assistant to help take some things off my hands that I was spending too much time on. This helped free me up to work on more important things, like making money.*

"In order to communicate effectively, one must know what is worth knowing and what is worth saying...and the difference between the two." **—James Halloran**

How To Cold Call

Rarely does it happen that a business starts up with a ready-made clientele and the phone ringing off the hook. Sooner or later, you're going to have to do some sales and legwork to recruit customers and sell them on why they should do business with you. Having experience in this field, we have a few tips for you.

Do some research before the call. This will have the effect of turning a "cold" call into a "warm" call. You don't have to stalk your potential customer or hire a private detective. It can be as simple as reading their website, getting a referral from a third party, mentioning a mutual acquaintance or discovering someone or something you have in common. Find that personal touch to get you a 'toe in the door' instead of being an annoying interruption.

Something else that can help is an actual premise or excuse to call, beyond '"I want you to consider using my business the next time you require my expertise." Perhaps you've gone to the same conference, have a mutual business, person, or interest in common, maybe a similar business or philosophical goal. But look for a "hook" that will interest the person and establish some rapport or trust, a reason to remember you and consider working together in the future.

After making the call to the best of your ability — and feel free to make a script or notes of some kind if you're nervous or afraid of blanking out, even to practice alone or with a trusted supportive friend or family member — make sure you follow up on the call at a later date.

And don't forget to ask for leads or referrals, while you're at it. While every call may not lead directly to work, it may provide an indirect but invaluable lead and get your name out there.

Scott Says: *Be sure to have a standard sales message you can deliver to a potential client. Target your market and talk to the people who make decisions, people with the power to move things forward.*

"Brevity is the soul of wit."
—William Shakespeare

The Elevator Pitch

You may have heard this before: you're in an elevator and you've only got a short time between floors to make an impression before the door opens again and people get out. It doesn't have to be an elevator, but there will be times where you meet people very briefly. Learn to seize these opportunities for networking.

So, an important skill set for promoting your business is the ability to give an appropriate sized pitch for whatever setting you're in. This is something that comes with forethought, practice, and research. Forethought means thinking hard about what your business is, why people might be interested in it, how to best explain it, and most of all, how to best sell it using as few words as possible. Practice your pitch in front of a mirror, using cue cards if needed, until you feel confident.

Then practice your elevator pitch with supportive friends or family. You want to be able to smoothly, and concisely, touch on all the important aspects of what you do, and the unique selling features of your business. You want to give a complete stranger a compelling reason to do business with you in future.

Besides a quick elevator sell, you also want to have enough information for those longer situations — if the elevator gets stuck between floors, or you're somewhere that's more conducive to a more leisurely conversation. This is where research comes in; you need to fully understand what you're doing in the following four areas. Know your business — every aspect of it that you can discover. Know your market — who is most likely to need your services, when, why, and in what price range? Know your competitors and what they have to offer. Know the trends - find out what new developments and trends there are in your field and try to learn more about the industry or business your clients may be in.

For every concise point you make, you should also have an expanded answer with further information in reserve, in case the time or interest presents itself. You want to be able to speak at length when you have the opportunity to do so, and really own the topic. Your fluid presentation, interest and passion, and depth of knowledge will come across quickly to make that great first impression you'll never have a second chance at.

Jeff Says: *When I meet somebody new and they ask what I do, I always try to answer them in the most efficient way possible so as to respect their time. If they want to ask questions from there, then I can easily get into specifics about my business.*

"Comfort zones are most often expanded through discomfort." – **Peter McWilliams**

Conference Networking 101

Conferences are a great place to not only renew your vision, be inspired, and gain knowledge, but to make new contacts inside and outside your industry — other business people who share similar interests and specialties. Network! The challenge is to go outside your personal comfort zone and actively try to meet people.

Everybody is basically in the same boat: terrified to start a conversation with a random person. Be the brave one and initiate the conversation. There's no risk — strangers are only friends you haven't met.

Another way to push yourself out of your comfort zone is to sit with people you don't know, even if you've come with friends. This can be hard, because if you've all travelled together or planned to meet up, the easier choice is to remain together. So if you just can't be separated, then choose a place to sit with other people and include them in the conversation.

Treat everyone as an equal. You never know who you're talking to so be nice, stay interested and ask lots of questions. This person could be anywhere in the world but they are here and spending time talking to you. Give them the attention they deserve.

Take the initiative to say hello to your heroes. Conferences give us a chance to see, in person, the industry experts and leaders in our community. Most of the micro-celebrities in your industry will be happy to give advice. Ask and you may be surprised. You've spent the money to get there so you might as well make it count. Beyond approaching the "experts", push yourself to get up at an open mic to showcase and share your experiences, or pose a good question. If you've always dreamed about being interviewed on a popular blog or podcast, why not try to arrange it?

Jeff Says: *As an entrepreneur I've learned time and time again that the broader your network is, the better it can be for business and personal growth.*

"It is not the event, but rather it is an interpretation of it that causes an emotional reaction." **—Albert Ellis**

Present Yourself Well

How people perceive you will affect how likely they are to do business with you. How you act is how you will be treated. So you need to first of all perceive yourself as a successful businessperson, a leader in your sector, and a unique and gifted person who has a lot to offer. Self-esteem is everything — if you've got it, people will sense and respect that. You don't need to be cocky or loud or arrogant, a quiet solid air of competence and confidence will do quite nicely.

Make sure you're matching that internal confidence with a show of external confidence. Put on your best face... 'Look good, feel good,' as they say. You don't have to spend a million bucks to look like a million bucks, but when you have a clean, neat appearance you are showing respect to yourself and others. Appearances do matter, and books do get judged by their cover — so make your book cover display the valuable contents as best you can.

Treat people with interest and respect at all times; these could be future friends or clients. Remember, you are a walking advertisement for your business — you want to do your best to promote the most positive perception of you and your business that you can.

But don't overdo it — nobody likes a phony. Stay authentic to who and what you are, at all times. Be yourself, the best self you can be; nobody else can be a better you, than you. Know that as you go about your work each day, you are making dreams come true for yourself and those around you, and be as positive as you can at all times. You will find that the right attitudes will attract business and the kind of people you want to work with.

Scott Says: *Use your credentials to open the doors but also make sure you can deliver what you say you can, and back it up with testimonials and references.*

"One comes to believe whatever one repeats to oneself sufficiently, whether the statement be true or false."
—Robert Collier

Being Great Is Pointless If Nobody Knows

You can be the most talented, skilled, efficient, cost-efficient provider of your specific service in the business, but without strong marketing and promotion, your business won't get off the ground. You need exposure. You need contacts. You need hype.

There are many ways to get the word out, depending on who your target market is. And nowadays many of them are free or accessible, as well as cost-effective. The personal face-to-face is always the best, but is labour-intensive. Phone calls and emails can add that personal touch. Building a buzz with social networking, webpages, or blogs is also an effective way to reach your audience. Do your research and think through a good marketing plan. Study market strategies, or pay attention to what others are doing in similar business situations.

But make it a priority. You don't want to be the best kept secret in town, you want the word to get out. Whenever you have a successful business interaction, ask your clients to refer you to others if they are pleased. You can create an incentive-based program for this if it seems practical, but most people are happy to spread the good news for free. Be careful, the reverse is also true — you don't want a marketing nightmare where you tick off a reporter who does a 10 week series on just how bad you are. So do your best to make every transaction have a happy ending — the only thing that spreads faster than good news is bad news.

Consider doing short demos, video clips, or introductory offers if you have a business that will encourage repeat customers. Get creative with your business cards to make them stand out. Use the unique nature of your business to market what is special about it. Make contacts with online and paper-based journals and see if you can get featured or interviewed — free press is awesome. And whatever method you decide to use for marketing, realize that it is an investment in present and future business.

Scott Says: *I found out early in my self-employment that you need to continuously self-promote and not feel bad about it. You need to put yourself on the map!*

"People never improve unless they look to some standard or example higher and better than themselves."

—Tyron Edwards

Choose Role Models Within Your Business Path

Asking for help or advice isn't a sign of weakness, but a sign of strength. And most business leaders, by the nature of their leadership, are generous in giving advice to others following in their path. As for a beginner in the business, the truly wise can learn from other people's mistakes, successes, and experiences and save themselves valuable time and energy by following good advice and stellar example.

Not only can you benefit from their advice and mentorship, they may very well introduce you to other good contacts in the industry and provide a path for you to follow. There's no need to reinvent the wheel, and we all need role models — so choose someone you admire, and explore the possibilities.

Even if you can't access the heroes you want to in person, you may be able to at least meet them at industry conferences and events — go up and talk to them. They are just human beings, after all, so treat them like you would want to be treated. Tell them specifically what you admire about their work, or ask an intelligent question if you have the opportunity. Reading about them on their websites or in magazines or biographies can be useful, too. You're looking for those little nuggets of hard-won knowledge that can help you along your path, or give you goals and examples.

Copying others isn't a bad thing. Forget that saying "don't be a copycat", there are times when it is entirely appropriate. Besides, you won't be a copycat because your job is to be uniquely you. It's okay to get a little help and inspiration along the way; you're still the one that's going to be putting in all the work. But, if you're lucky enough to build a solid regular mentorship with a leader in the industry, you'll have someone to bounce ideas off of, someone who is cheering for you, and someone who can encourage you and keep you accountable to your own goals.

Scott Says: *I find myself rotating role models who I wish to be like, because depending where I am at in my career there are some who I wish to be like for different reasons. There may come a time too when you surpass your role models.*

"Knowing others is wisdom, knowing yourself is enlightenment." —**Lao-tzu**

Your Competitors Are Not The Competition

We are always cordial with our competitors, largely because we don't see them strictly as 'competitors'. Not only does this assure we have less drama in our life, but also means we are alive to opportunities where possibly we can work collaboratively together. Additionally, with a shared specialty and interests, it is likely you will see them at the same conferences, outlets, and events you attend, so get to know them and treat them with respect.

That is not to advocate being naive. There will be some merely interested in meeting with you to advance only themselves, or to see if they should take you seriously as a competitor. But overall, it will always pay off to be friendly and informed about the competition that's out there. And look at it this way, if they're ever over-booked, they may be far more likely to pass extra business over to you, just for making that extra effort and being a decent human being. It doesn't cost anything to be nice!

Many businesses actually benefit from having many providers-of-service. Take lawyers for example (one lawyer in a town can just get by, but two lawyers can make a killing!) As long as you're in an industry that has a market, or can create a market, the sky's the limit. Business attracts business, and a colleague's wild success may very well carry over to your office as people start to pay more attention to your industry in general.

Don't assume that those who you see as 'competitors' are actually 'in competition' with you. Every business develops diverse types of relationships with their clientele differently, so internally your businesses may not work the same way. You may occasionally provide a missing piece for them, and vice versa. We have both been successful in undertaking partnership and joint business opportunities with other companies, big and small.

Remember, your competitors stay in business by looking at and being aware of any and all opportunities, being flexible and open to possibilities, as well as working hard. Once you understand what their objectives and method of operations are, you will be able to assess where your interests may merge, and what may become points of possible collaboration or joint projects.

For example, every business is interested in cutting costs by getting the best deal from vendors. One way is for a minimal order discount — where you team up to 'bulk buy', and both end up with savings. This could work with office supplies, fuel, or advertising. Always be aware of any strategy where you could team up with one or more competitors with the end result of increasing profits for both of you.

It may seem counter intuitive, but even if another business is doing work that you could be doing, the possibility is still there to create a more profitable 'joint venture' that at the end of the day serves everyone's best interests. There's just nothing wrong with win/win, is there?

Scott Says: *When I was teaching, Teachers were called associates. When I became an entertainer, people appeared to be very competitive. I called up several competitors who were further on in their careers and introduced myself and asked as many questions as they had time for. Some of those "competitors" I now call my close friends.*

"The most important motive for work in school and in life is pleasure in work, pleasure in its result, and the knowledge of the value of the result to the community."
—Albert Einstein

Partner With Like-Minded People

As the old saying goes, "Birds of a feather flock together," and this is good for both the individual bird, and the whole flock. When you surround yourself with people who have similar aspirations and goals, you can support each other in attaining them. This is much easier than constantly having to explain yourself, argue about your choices, or defend your lifestyle. Your energy is revitalized rather than depleted. You can cheerlead for each other, offer a sympathetic and understanding ear, and share successes. It doesn't have to be lonely at the top if you bring friends to the top along with you.

If you don't currently have a peer group of like-minded friends or colleagues, start looking.

You can try conferences and industry events, workshops or short courses, or maybe you will run into others when working with a supplier or client. Be friendly at all times, send out those vibes, and before you know it, you'll have found the kind of people you want to be with. (This is made easiest by BEING the kind of person that you want to be around.)

Besides going for the old standards that you're comfortable with, try diversifying the people you spend time with. You can learn new things, stretch yourself a bit and be more motivated as a result.

But choose wisely — you are who your friends are, and you want good influences. Nobody's perfect, but try to find people who are generally good role models, who lead balanced lives and are positive to be around. They don't have to be industry experts to qualify, although that doesn't hurt either.

Scott Says: *In business there are many ups and downs. Surround yourself with positive, motivated people who will support you when you are down and inspire you to take your ideas to the next level.*

"If you're serious about building your personal brand, there will be no time for Wii."
—Gary Vaynerchuk

Your Personal Brand

Your business is all about you — YOU are the product, the service, the front-facing person. So start thinking about yourself in terms of a product that is being offered and be the brand you want to see in the world. We have found that people don't hire companies — they hire people.

You need to take control of your 'brand' for your business or personal style, otherwise a number of forces you have no control over will be happy to do it for you, and without your permission and/or direction. You want to be the person who makes those decisions and choose the direction, method, and delivery of your brand — what it looks like, what it is, and where you find it.

The first place to control your brand is on-line and hopefully you already have done this to some extent. We live in a wired age and personal branding is now a part of business, politics and social interactions. So a good website or social networking representation can be key to staking out your territory and defining your brand space. Remember that the internet means you have the ability to speak daily to dozens, hundreds, or even thousands of people via social networking sites.

But you also need to be authentic in who and what you are; beyond your personal brand, you also need to maintain a personal touch. However, in being authentic also be strategic — only share what you're comfortable with. You are allowed to maintain privacy and personal boundaries, but sometimes by sharing yourself in at least a limited way, you can create a personal brand that is equity to be cashed in on at a later date.

Jeff Says: *I am surprised how many people have checked out my blog and twitter before meeting me in person. This has made it really easy to start conversations.*

"People never improve unless they look to some standard or example higher and better than themselves." **—Tyron Edwards**

Model Yourself After Successful Entrepreneurs

Imitation is the most sincere form of flattery — and it also makes a fine, fine business model when you're imitating success. You don't have to dress up in matching outfits, or change your name, but studying successful entrepreneurs and their methods is simply a safe shortcut to success. Learning from their failures can save you some time, pain, and money. Don't be afraid to ask questions of successes in the industry. What did, or didn't, work for them? What did they wish someone had told them when they were starting out?

Usually people are glad to think that their time and effort can be of help to others, that their lessons aren't wasted, that they, themselves, are worthy of imitation. It's flattering to be looked up to, gratifying to be recognized by peers, and it's also rewarding to be in a position where you can help others achieve success.

Of course, this principle isn't just one-sided. You might do the same, someday, for others who are starting out. We all have humble beginnings, born naked and able to do nothing but cry. Look how far you've come. Never forget that, nor the help you've received along the way. You have a debt that you can pay forward. When things come full-circle, it's your obligation, your duty, and your pleasure to mentor other people. Give back what you've been given so generously. It feels good!

Scott Says: *The best way I've found to check out your competition is at trade shows or conferences or conventions. It is a great way to strike up conversations and also study the promotional info they give out to the same customers that come to you.*

"It's not what you know, it's who you know."
—Unknown

It's All About Your Personal Network

If people don't know who you are, they can't hire you. So don't go hiding under rocks — it's your obligation to yourself and your business to get your name, face and website out there. Carry business cards with you. Start conversations with strangers. Unless you're in the shower or asleep, you're always 'on' — think of yourself as a walking billboard. Okay, you don't have to wear a sandwich board when you go get coffee, or tattoo an ad across your forehead, but remember that you're a business person and you're representing your business whether you're out in public, or in cyberspace, wherever.

Join online groups and forums that are relevant to your industry, join a gym, join a supportive community. Think about ways you can meet new people and make new connections. (It doesn't have to be just work-related to be a good contact.) Volunteering, sports, leisure pastimes, charitable fundraisers, and other community and social settings are all places where you may come across someone is interested in your line of work . And if they don't need your services they just might keep you in mind for someone they know who does.

Consider making a list of your friends and family and asking them individually, or via a mass mail-out, for leads or word-of-mouth promotion. As they say, it's not always 'what' you know but 'who' you know. And everybody knows somebody. Who is more likely to want you to succeed than those close to you? People always like to work with businesses that in some way have a personal connection — there is a built-in level of implied trust if you know them, or know someone they know.

So, even if you're just taking the bus or waiting in a grocery store line-up, start a friendly conversation. Opportunities are everywhere, and you never know who you're standing next to.

Jeff Says: *When I think about the active projects in my business, I can always trace them back to an event I went to where I met somebody who either hired me or introduced me to somebody else. Or both.*

"Most of us ask for advice when we know the answer but we want a different one."
—Ivern Ball

Ask For Advice, But Follow Your Own Instincts

Family, friends, and role models can be a valuable resource when it comes to making decisions. People are usually flattered to be asked their opinion and it is often helpful to get fresh perspective on a challenge, new situation, or change in direction. Going through the pros and cons of a scenario can be easier with a good sounding board, but the best advice is often the advice you give yourself when you're talking with someone you trust and respect.

Good advice is priceless, and bad advice is an opportunity to learn to trust yourself. So take the advice of others when it seems to fit; but always go with your gut. Never underestimate hunches, gut feelings, and intuition. Learning to trust those leads will pay off.

Scott Says: *Running ideas by a family member, even if they don't know my industry, is a strategy I use because I find I need to verbalize the creative idea that I just received.*

"Learning how to learn is life's most important skill." **—Tony Buzan**

If You Don't Know How, Learn!

Nobody goes into business knowing it all. And we've already dealt with situations where you can delegate tasks that you can't stand, or are not as efficient at. But what about situations where there is something you just haven't come across yet, or something else you were planning to learn but hadn't yet? Our advice to you is that in your own business, consider yourself always at 'on the job training.' Half the fun of running your own business is that, besides specializing in something you enjoy doing, you can also add growth and variety and an opportunity to develop new skills.

So, if you're asked to do something that you have yet to attempt, say 'Sure thing!' then figure out how to get it done. Whether that involves reading a certain book, doing an online tutorial, trial and error, taking a class or asking another specialist in the field for advice — knowledge is power. And wisdom is knowing when and how to acquire and use that power. You might spend some extra time in educating yourself, but think of it as an investment for the future and the chance to do something the following time with increased skill and proficiency.

It feels good to empower yourself by learning something new. Nothing is more motivating than having a client, a deadline, and an exciting new skill. It may be frustrating your first time out, but be patient with yourself. Roll your sleeves up, remind yourself that you are a skilled and talented person who is a beginner in this particular task, and don't give up. The best way to learn something is hands-on — being paid to do it is just an added bonus.

Remember: you are a human being with limitless potential and infinite possibility. The only requirement to tap those possibilities and potentials is time, patience, and belief.

Jeff Says: *I have pretty much based my entire business on this principle: If I don't know how to do something I will figure it out or find somebody that can!*

"Remarkable claims require remarkable proof." —**Carl Sagan**

Always Ask, "What Would A Professional Do?"

Even though you are a professional, it can be easy to forget that at times, especially when you're first starting out. Not many of us begin with the mentality that we are experts, not amateurs, in our fields. So remember to ask yourself, especially when you have decisions to make, equipment to purchase, or an important presentation to do: "How would a professional handle this?" You will make better decisions, and provide a better quality of service if you follow this simple guideline, and treat yourself and others accordingly.

Do everything the right way — and there usually is a right, and wrong, way to do things, or at least a 'good' and 'less good' way. The right way is the way of the professional; we all start out as amateurs, but the sooner you leave that mentality behind, the sooner you reach the ranks of the pro.

This also goes for your appearance, your promotional materials and your equipment. When you look and feel good, you put your best face forward, project confidence in your work, and produce quality in your business. This is another case of the investment of time or money being justified by the result.

Pay money for things that matter — you don't need diamond cuff links to impress people, or flashy items you have no idea how to use — but the tools of your trade should be ones that are high-quality. Usually higher-quality items pay for themselves not only in making you look and feel professional, but in the performance they yield. Quality purchases should generally be more efficient, more durable, have better service and warranties, and also be more dependable. This isn't always the case. Sometimes you are paying for nothing but a brand name or really expensive advertising campaigns, so be discerning. When there's no difference between brand-name and no-name and it's a minor purchase, by all means go for the best deal. But the old saying "you get what you pay for" can often bear out, over time. And unreliable equipment that fails or needs frequent replacement or repair, costs you time, which costs you money, and can even cost you your reputation — and your business.

Why take the risk? You're a pro — act the part.

Scott Says: *To make myself and my business stand out I always make decisions that I think the best person in the industry would make. Then, I usually follow what my decision is... if it is within the budget.*

"Learn to get in touch with the silence within yourself, and know that everything in this life has purpose." **—Elizabeth Kübler-Ross**

Make Time For Learning

Be proactive in educating yourself in your field, don't wait until you need specialized knowledge to acquire it. Most people learn better when they're not under the gun from a client, rush job or an emergency. And since you have chosen a profession that you enjoy, are good at, and is interesting to you, keep those fires alive by constantly learning new things. Just build that space into your work week or your annual schedule — what teachers call their "lesson time". It is refreshing to learn a new lesson in how to do something, and it will pay off in keeping you up-to-date and motivated.

You don't have to do it completely on your own. Different people learn differently so find out what works best for you and what your learning style is. You can mix it up a bit, too. Take workshops, courses, training, or certification in your field. Take some first-aid while you're at it. That's a good skill set to have in any business, and could save a life. Subscribe to newsletters, blogs or twitter accounts in the industry — any format that is fresh and enjoyable and will keep you on the leading edge of new developments. Make time for shop-talk with other professionals, or go on a 'field trip' to see something new.

When you're a life-long learner, you're never bored. Learning is often different when you're an adult than when you're a kid, because if you were taught in a typical classroom, you didn't get to choose what you learned. You followed the government curriculum as administered by the resources selected by your school board, as taught in the lesson plans developed by your teacher. Now's your chance to get a real education, one that you own and love. Because you get to pick what you're learning and interested in, and the whens, hows, wheres, and whats of that learning. It's on your terms, on your time, and in the way that plays to your individual strengths and interests.

Scott Says: *I try to read online news everyday and research what's happening in the industry. Knowing what current issues are helps me make better choices for future directions to go in.*

"This is how nature works — evolution doesn't linger on past failures, it's always building on what works."
– Quote from Rework, by Jason Fried & David Heinemeier Hansson

Learn From Success More Than From Failures

It's okay to fail — we already covered that — but when you fail, and you've more or less figured out why, don't dwell on it. Save that kind of thinking for success, not failure. Feel free to dwell on past successes when you need encouragement because that is reinforcing what you did right in the past, helping you feel presently successful, and setting you up for future success.

Think of a baby learning to walk. They may cry for a minute if they hurt themselves, but generally they get over it and keep trying. They wobble along until eventually they no longer remember what being unsteady was like.

Now imagine a baby who acted like some of us adults do, drowning in constant self-criticism. This baby would sit on the floor playing back the falls, analyzing why they happened, or how to perhaps avoid them, or if there might be a pattern. This baby would do only the safest thing — crawl, or cruise on furniture. This baby might even try walking alone, but carefully sit down as soon as things looked precarious. In short, this baby might not ever learn to walk, because this baby was cursed with insecurity, fear of failure, over-analysis, and not being able to walk perfectly on the first try. This baby learned all the wrong lessons from one experience of falling, focusing on failure only, instead of all the successful steps that came before — preventing any more successful steps from following. That is negative backwards thinking, like staring glumly at the only cloud in an otherwise blue sky; it is as futile as trying to make constellations out of the black parts of the sky, instead of using the brightly-lit stars to "connect the dots".

Now imagine coaching a baby to walk. Do you say, "You stupid kid. You took three steps, but then you fell on the fourth one. Give up already." No! You encourage, clap, cheer, break out the camera, and call others into the room. You count each wobbly step or growing distance as a new victory. If this is your first child, the first step probably merits several phone calls, or a ten-minute entry in the baby book, and endless praise, kisses, and cheers.

And that's the kind of attitude you still deserve for all your efforts — applaud each victory, replay each success, emphasize everything done well. Pat yourself on the back when you persevere. Don't become an egotistical maniac who believes they're never wrong. Just don't wallow in your mistakes; be grateful when things go well for you, then keep going in that direction.

People respond much better to praise than criticism — and that includes you, when you're talking to yourself. You'll perform better, you'll learn faster, and you'll be happier.

Jeff Says: *What we mostly learn from failing is what doesn't work. It is better to find out what DOES work and discover ways to repeat success, not failure.*

"Opportunity is missed by most people because it is dressed in overalls and looks like work." **—Thomas Edison**

See A Need, Fill A Need

Your business will only exist if there is a market for it. If you're selling sand at the beach, no marketing plan, introductory offer or expert sales pitch is going to help you out. So analyze your industry, come up with a need that isn't being filled or a problem that needs a better solution than the options that currently exist, and provide that to your clients.

Needs can range from products to services, to advice and counseling. Needs are, in fact, endless, and so are the solutions to those needs. While you can possibly just come up with a list of things people 'might' need, it's best to find out what people actually need. You can outright ask people what their needs are, then develop a response to those needs. Or even better, fill one of your own needs because there's a good chance there's more than a few people who will require the same thing.

Ditto for problems. The only thing more satisfying than solving your own, is solving the problems of others (okay, you can't necessarily solve everyone's problems, but you can probably help with the industry-related ones.) Think through complications that plague you in your line of work, develop solutions or fixes, and begin offering solutions.

If you stop to consider it, this really is the underlying reason for every business out there. Those businesses that have a harder time of things are usually selling things that aren't necessarily needed (so they have to invest in creating a need, or convincing others of that need) or are creating more problems than they solve.

Jeff Says: *Any time I launch a new app I am primarily trying to fulfill one of my own needs first.*

"There are no mistakes, no coincidences. All events are blessings given to us to learn from." **—Elizabeth Kübler-Ross**

Money Can't Buy Me Love

Money doesn't buy happiness. It buys time; time well-spent buys happiness. Money is a means to an end, not the end itself. If you spend money like it's going out of fashion, it will go out of fashion. As in, you won't have it in any fashion whatsoever. No matter how much you make, if you overspend, you are worse off than if you had never started in the first place, because you risk losing everything, including your good name, your business, your family and reputation. Not only will you lose everything you bought including the roof over your head, you will have wasted all the time and effort you put into earning that money in the first place. So, instead of using all your cash up in a whirlwind of constantly updated gadgets, or the latest model sports car, or the —est anything (fastest, newest, flashiest, you name it!) — use it to buy the one commodity every person wants more of when they get to the end of the line. Time.

Time with your loved ones. Time to do valuable things that feed your heart, your mind, your body, your spirit, even if they don't draw a paycheque. Time to see the world a bit, even if it's just a leisurely stroll to another neck of the woods, a backpacking trip near or far away, or a fishing trip with your grandfather. Time to rest, recuperate, and rejuvenate so that you can work productively and happily. Time to listen to the birds, see the flowers and the trees, enjoy Creation and your limited time offer on our quickly-spinning earth.

There is no paycheque big enough to buy away regret, and no business or store that sells happiness by the bushel, barrel, bucket, or teaspoon. So think hard about what you do with your money and with the time it can buy for you. It's better to share it wisely within your friends and family and community, than pour it down the drain on junk you don't need.

Scott Says: *Working holidays are a win-win for my family and me. I try to celebrate victories by turning work off when I can and inviting the family on the cool work trips that I get to go on.*

"Luck is what happens when preparation meets opportunity." **–Seneca**

Rain Making

Rain making — creating customer workflow — is key. Customers don't aimlessly call or randomly email, hoping to stumble onto someone who can solve their problems. It's your job to bring in new customers and projects to feed your business so it can grow and thrive. While it may be obvious and rarely disputed that without customers you have no business, many new entrepreneurs seem to forget this basic truth — at their peril.

This is most common after the completion of your first major project that gives you breathing space and money for a few months. There is a temptation to sit around, spend it, go to the beach, or whatever. This is when the seeds for disaster are being planted; they are laid in the good times. Then, when there is an economic downturn or too many corners have been cut, there are no checks and balances in place. When times are good you still need to keep other irons in the fire, put in proposals for the future, and so on.

How do you make rain? Giving good service at a fair price is a great place to start. Client relationships that last are the best foundation for any business. Those relationships are built on ongoing attention to client need and providing workable suggestions on how your clients can exceed their goals.

Next, establish methods to let your potential customers know what you do and why they should hire you. This includes networking at trade shows, conferences, professional groups and online communities.

Consider creating opportunities to share your knowledge at conferences or workshops, which can mean an immediate fee, plus future work. You are in business because you have learned something that is 'of use' to others. Contact conference organizers and tell them how and why you can contribute to the success of their next conference. Or organize your own seminar or conference.

Use the media as a tool. If you don't know how, learn. If you can't find someone in your area to teach you, embrace this as a further business opportunity and, later, educate others who find themselves in the same boat

Ask people to hire you or use your services. If they don't use you now, they may in future. Also, they may be asked by someone else for a referral in your line of work. It's called networking. Casting your net wide works.

Finally, as our parents used to say, we've two ears for a reason, so ask questions, then stop talking and listen. Then ask more questions so you are sure you understand, then respond to your clients' needs.

Jeff Says: *You always have to make it rain. When it's dry you have to make it rain, and when you are in a downpour you need to be working on making it rain the next day.*

"To give real service you must add something which cannot be bought or measured with money, and that is sincerity and integrity." **—Douglas Noel Adams**

Freebies and Giveaways

Big stores like Costco can afford to give away loads of free samples to introduce product to customers and entice people to stay and shop longer (everybody loves free stuff!) You can use this technique too, but unless you have the buying power of a corporation like Costco, don't get too carried away. Just offer enough to tempt new customers to do business with you, or old customers to do more business with you. Use it as leverage for repeat business, or new business. You can't work for free for long — you'll go broke. Everyone has overhead, and everyone deserves to be paid a respectable wage for their work.

Doing too much for free not only deprives you of a just wage, but can lessen your perceived value or undercut your competitors and your industry in general. Creating market expectation from clients that your services can be had for cheap might create the illusion that the services are not worth paying for. Ever. So don't shoot yourself in the foot with this one. Balance is always the key.

Having said that — sometimes free, under-priced, or generous/charitable pro bono work can lead to future paying work. If even the cut-throat legal industry throws in freebies now and then, it can't be all bad, right? So you need to use your judgment: is it likely, or even possible, that a freebie now may lead to paying work later? (You can even ask this question outright, if you have a good client relationship.)

Unless you're using this as a technique to drum up business because you have absolutely NONE, and you need the experience and exposure desperately, try to make sure you're already making your minimum costs and not turning away good-paying steady work in order to perform the low-service or no-charge jobs. Only when you have it made and there are piles of money under every mattress in the house, then find a safe place to bank, and do all the free work you like.

Scott Says: *Usually, when I give free products and services away I am gaining something: A charitable tax receipt, TV footage that I can add to my website, or some excellent referrals by people who have tried my hypnosis audio CDs.*

"Kindness is more than deeds. It is an attitude, an expression, a look, a touch. It is anything that lifts another person."
—C. Neil Strait

The Best Place To Get New Work: Existing Customers

Constantly chasing fresh customers and re-selling and re-establishing yourself is not the most efficient way to do business (unless you're in the type of business where your client only needs you once. Like lifetime-guaranteed cast-iron silicon-coated doorstops.) If things are slow, or even merely steady, do check in with your existing clientele. Create a system where you follow-up. Do your customers need anything right now? If not, is there perhaps something new you can find to offer them? Are they happy with the work you did? You already have an established relationship, after all — a rapport, a trust level, a mutually beneficial relationship. So every subsequent positive transaction or communication only serves to strengthen that bond, and leaves them more satisfied and more likely to continue being repeat customers. Working with existing clientele is what's known in business as a "hot lead" versus a "cold lead". Makes sense that existing clients are going to "warm up" faster to doing business with you again — why not help them make you a hard habit to break?

Your customers will likely appreciate your checking in on them. Customer service and that personal touch, a level of relationship in business, are things that can't be bought. Not only is it good manners, but good business sense.

Make sure you keep track of all your customers — via database, a little black book, a printout, a calendar, or the old "rolodex" — and regularly check in with them, to make sure everything is going well, and to see if there's anything else they may want or need. It saves them the trouble of having to look you up, and it makes them feel appreciated and well looked- after. You don't have to sound like you're desperately trying to drum up work — just a friendly email will do the trick. : "Hey — just thinking of my favourite customer today, how's everything working? Anything you need?" You don't need to fly overhead with a plane banner, or mail out special brochures and surveys. Try to maintain as personal a touch as you can, and avoid overdoing it — you don't want to turn your hot leads cold. You want to work effectively while keeping the client base you've got. Make sure they are happy before you worry about bringing in new business. Not only will you grow your business in a solid, manageable way, but also more efficiently.

Because with a loyal client base, word tends to spread, and new jobs come looking for you instead of the other way around.

Scott Says: *My email newsletter has been one of the best ways to stay connected with my old clients. Usually, every time I send the newsletter out I get a booking!*

"The path to success is to take massive, determined action." **—Tony Robbins**

Do You Take The Gig?

Just because you're in business doesn't mean you have to say "yes" to every person who has the ability to send an e-mail or dial 7 to 10 consecutive digits, correctly. It's okay to sort through business opportunities. Don't take too much time or you will lose business and get a bad reputation, and don't do it for a bad reason like, "I don't feel like working today," but you will have to pick and choose. Do it professionally, and do it wisely, but do it. Don't over-extend yourself and ruin your business by "biting off more than you can chew" or repeatedly taking on jobs you regret.

First, remember the fundamentals of business: (money in) - (money out) = profit. What remains is what you get to keep. Money is a measurement for any project, but it isn't the only one. However, a business that is spending more or almost as much as it costs to do business is not a sustainable model. Be aware of this at all times and know your 'bottom line' to keep afloat. The following considerations have also served us well:

The gig has to be with people we want to work with.

Can we do the job, or do we have too many other commitments? — Saying yes but then short-changing that job or others, or having to later decline or postpone a commitment is essentially robbing your customer, and ultimately, your business and your reputation. Better an honest no, than a yes that later turns into a "not really", "not now" or a "no, not ever", wasting everyone's time and potentially creating hard feelings as well as inconvenience all around. Protect your reputation!

It has to be interesting. — Not everything is a 10 on the excitement scale, but make sure you're not constantly doing jobs you hate, or you'll grow to resent your business.

It has to contain a level of challenge, so that we can learn from the project as an extra benefit to our business. — Sure, doing easy things is occasionally okay, but growth is where it's at.

Does this project afford an opportunity to learn about an area, or subject, new to us, that may result in additional diversity of work down the road and give us a strategic advantage? Look to the future, expand horizons and keep one finger on the pulse of your technologies and potential developments down the road. Keep an open mind!

Is it worth it financially and will the client be able to pay the bill? — This is where we started, but it bears repeating. It's great to do what you love, but it's greater to get paid for doing what you love, especially if that is your livelihood and your means of supporting yourself and others.

Not every question must be answered with a yes, but it is a good starting point when we are deciding — do we take the gig or not? If doubt exists, it is an indicator that we need to ask more questions and examine the situation. At the end of the day, trust your intuition and go with your heart.

Jeff Says: *My number one consideration when choosing projects to work on is if I like the people.*

"It's not the time you put in, but what you put in the time." **—Burg's Philosophy**

The Work/Life Balance

The best model we have found for balance is in the teachings of the medicine wheel. While the sacred teachings vary, the circle holds all things; within the circle balance must be maintained in the four quarters representing, among other things, mind, body, spirit, and emotion. This carries over into your business. When you are balanced physically, emotionally, spiritually, and mentally, you are a well-rounded person. It takes effort and care to keep each domain healthy.

In business, the same teachings apply. You need to put effort into your equipment and surroundings (physical), your relationships with your suppliers or clients (emotional), your integrity and attitude (spiritual), and be mindful of working efficiently and intelligently (mental).

Beyond that, you also want to ensure that work does not take over your life, but is only one aspect of it. The medicine wheel teaches overall balance, but is also circular because we are walking a path that goes full circle as we learn. We travel the four seasons as the earth spins, and we travel through our own life seasons. Be aware that there is more to life than just work.

Try actually tracking time spent in an hour, day, week, or month and assess it in terms of balance in each of these areas. Check that family, friends, outside interests, and self-care in all four areas get the attention they deserve. Ask others for advice in attaining balance, and be mindful of this need. Try to build balance in so that it becomes automatic pieces of time already allocated to the important parts of your life.

We are each allotted only so many hours on this earth, billable or otherwise. Try to live a balanced life that is going to result in a minimum of regret and a maximum amount of satisfaction when you look back from that final hour on earth — whenever it may arrive. Very few of us know the time or place of that hour but we all know that one day it will come. An important thing to keep in mind, and a good way to keep your priorities straight.

Jeff Says: *Keeping balance between the mental, physical, emotional and spiritual aspects of life is tough but worthwhile in maintaining overall happiness.*

"Call it a clan, call it a network, call it a tribe, call it a family. Whatever you call it, whoever you are, you need one."

—Jane Howard

Family First!

The people in your life, especially your immediate family, should always take priority. However, part of that balance involves providing for them, especially your dependants, whoever they may be. So it is not as cut and dry as immediately dropping everything and spending every waking moment with the ones you love. You also need to have the means to support them, feed them, clothe them, keep a roof over them and pay the bills. So by working, you are putting your family first. Make sure they know that, and make sure you know that, too.

Don't confuse working for a living with work being your whole life. There is no point in making millions if you miss every major (and minor) event in your family's life and they justifiably resent you for it. When you draw up your calendar and schedule, put your family events first, if you can. This helps you align your priorities and will make you (and your family) happier and more successful.

Your clients and colleagues have families too, and will not only understand, but respect that you put your family first. And if they don't respect that, either they need more examples of it in their lives, or else you don't need a business relationship with them. Priorities are important, and good priorities are universal.

Another way to keep your family at the forefront is to keep them involved and updated as to progress. Celebrate with them! Create traditions to reward one another when a new level of success is reached in business. It can be a special family night, a trip, even a special meal. But keep your most important "business partners" in the loop, and celebrate your business success with those who matter most — the people you're actually working for, 24/7.

Jeff Says: *Working from home helps me balance work and life. It's great to be able to eat breakfast, lunch and dinner with my family — and still put in a full day's work.*

"I want to be as famous as Persil Automatic"
—Victoria Beckham (Posh Spice)

Be The "Go-To" Person Or Company

To stand out in business, and to succeed — you want to be the 'go to' guru. You want clients to think of you when they require your niche service or product. Establishing yourself as a leader means providing the best service or product you can, maintaining a positive and respectful relationship and rapport with your clients and staying on top of industry trends and developments. Make it your goal to continually improve, and provide maximum satisfaction to your clients. There's no need to consider the competition when you are competing with yourself every day to become better, faster, stronger, smarter, more successful at what you do. Do your best, and then better it with practice.

Take pride in the work you do. This doesn't mean boasting or taking out a billboard bragging about being number one. It means being able to say to yourself and your loved ones that no matter what size of job you had or how much or little you were paid for it, you did your best and put your best effort, your heart, and your back into it.

Stay humble and approachable, look for feedback from your clients. Ask them what you did right, and then ask them where they'd like to see improvements. Good two-way conversations and a high level of trust, honesty, and communication are invaluable to any business.

Keep in touch with your customers. And whether it's from e-mails, ads, fridge magnets, or pens with your phone number on it, keep your name out there and in front of them. When they have a business need that you can provide, you want to be the first person they think of.

Jeff Says: *When my customers think "web stuff", I want to be the first person they think of!*

"You know the difference between you and me? I make this look GOOD."
—Will Smith, Men in Black

Dress For Success

When you look good, you feel good. And when you feel good, you 'do' good. So make sure you're always putting your best foot forward. Shower in the morning, and wear something that puts you in a working mood, whatever makes you feel good. Some people prefer button up shirts, others prefer t-shirts.

People who work from home get a pretty sweet deal: pants are optional. When you first start working from home, you may joke about sitting in your underwear while taking a client call or wake up by noon and work all night. That may be cool for a while but will eventually get old. It's also too easy to wake up and get stuck in work right away before even grabbing something to eat, let alone get dressed. Half the day can pass before you hop in the shower, get dressed and get motivated. After a while it can feel like the days drag on and on.

Besides looking good for clients, you need to look good for you. You're giving your body physical and visual signals that this is "work" time, wearing apparel that makes it easiest for you to perform your work, and signaling to yourself and to anyone else who sees you that you take this work seriously and believe in the value of your business, and yourself.

Jeff Says: *My morning ritual includes having a shower and putting on a button-up shirt and jeans to get me into work mode.*

"I like to pay taxes. With them I buy civilization."
—Oliver Wendell Holmes, Jr.

Taxes Are A Fact Of Business Life

Everyone's heard about the two inevitable and unavoidable things in life — death, and taxes. So while you're keeping busy at staying alive, don't neglect the taxman, because it's guaranteed he won't forget you. Doing taxes, especially for a small business or as a self-employed entrepreneur, can be onerous and there are a lot of tricks of the trade, so the best advice is to get yourself a "tax guru" who knows everything there is to know. Meet with them to set up a system — ideally way before tax time when they're busy and you're stressed out over the deadline — and follow it to the best of your ability.

You need to deal with GST, income tax, and perhaps other deductions. If you are working from home, there are certain parts of your overhead that may be deductible. If you use your vehicle for work, you need to track mileage and fuel and repair costs regularly. Receipts (and the organizing of them) are important. There are a lot of details worth knowing, and a good tax advisor can make your bookwork and organization relatively pain free. If you're completely hopeless at bookwork and show up with a cardboard shoebox packed full of papers, they can probably fix that too — just expect to pay a bit more for the extra service.

Tax advisors can also help counsel you on your investments and savings, as well as give advice on RRSP's. There are high- and low-interest savings accounts. Savings are an important part of business, and a really good habit to get into.

The best thing about having a tax advisor or accountant is that second-person perspective they give to your business, at arm's length. The person spending your money shouldn't be the person counting your money.

Scott Says: *I like to have two credit cards: one for personal and one for business. This creates less confusion when my bookkeeper is doing my bookkeeping during tax time.*

"A players hire A+ players, but B players hire C, C hire D. If you start down this slippery slope, you'll soon end up with Z players; this is called The Bozo Explosion" **—Guy Kawasaki**

When To Outsource Or Sub-Contract

If you need help getting work done, always hire A+ people. You want to work with the best of the best — because birds of a feather flock together, and being considered an expert by association is just one of the side benefits. You also stand to gain good service and good advice.

Sometimes working with the best costs more, but just as with products and supplies — you get what you pay for. Paying an expensive expert who works fast and knows what they're doing often saves money as opposed to waiting around while an amateur learns the ropes on your hourly billed invoice.

So now that you know who to hire (the best!) — what about when? A good rule of thumb is to hire someone when it is ultimately going to either save, or make, money for you. Perhaps by freeing you to do other things (like make more money) or by providing additional services that expand your business horizons or enable you to serve your clients better.

Jeff Says: *Not only has hiring A+ people allowed me to work with some amazing talented people, it has also made me some great friends for life.*

"Be kind whenever possible. It is always possible." **—Buddhist Quote**

Never Write A Nasty Email

In business, we all deal with people who are difficult and challenge our patience. All of us have responded with offence, anger and frustration, but it is always a mistake to write an email which is vicious, mean, condescending, or cruel. Writing a sarcastic email may feel good in the moment, but it is a transitory pleasure that doesn't last. And frankly, the type of person who caused you to write the email likely won't be changed as a result, so there's not much point if you're hoping to modify their behaviour.

This temporary venting of a negative emotion will come back and haunt you months or years later, and could end up costing you and your business political, social, and financial resources. The person you blast today may be your boss down the road, or sitting on a funding board making decisions about your company. And if they aren't, they may be friends of the people who are. People don't remember professional emails that get things done. Those serve their purpose and are forgotten. What they will remember are emails and comments that offend them, and they are more likely to share them with others, so why ruin your reputation in a moment?

Don't let other people's issues reduce you. Grow and learn instead of falling into bad patterns or knee-jerk reactions. Step back or walk away. Take a deep breath and wait until you can think clearly. And if you need to write it out, do that somewhere private where you can shred or burn it afterwards.

Stop, breathe, think . . . before you press the 'send' key. Remember, it is easier to stay out of trouble then to get out of trouble.

Jeff Says: *Decisions made in fear or anger are rarely good decisions.*

"Passion is energy. Feel the power that comes from focusing on what excites you."
— Oprah Winfrey

Invest Your Energy Appropriately

To maintain your personal power and remain centered and balanced, pay attention to where you place your energy. Don't give it away needlessly or heedlessly. Anything or anyone that consumes your time, money, energy, or focus is accessing your energy. You are the one who is in charge of that energy and you need to be responsible for it, one hundred per cent.

Be aware of your boundaries and limitations and be on guard against poor choices that disempower you and your business. Emotional, mental, spiritual, and physical energy needs to be invested just as wisely as your time and your money. The more consciously you invest that energy — and stop giving it away foolishly or in ways that drain you — the better a position you will be in, at all times, personally and in business.

Negativity is everywhere and it is easy to become discouraged, angry, pessimistic, or frustrated. But these are all things that take away power, rather than retaining it. Positivity, calm and patience all serve to give you power and help you hold on to it. Whether you meditate, go for a walk, take control of your schedule, or counsel with someone you trust — do what it takes to retain power over the only thing you have power over — you.

Scott Says: *Know that the only behaviour you can change is your own. Have a positive and healthy lifestyle and don't worry about others and whatever jealously or envy they may direct towards you directly, or indirectly.*

"We make the assumption that everyone sees life the way we do."
— Don Miguel Ruiz (The Four Agreements)

Dealing With Complaints

This is where your culture of 'good manners' will pay off. Sooner or later, you will get a complaint from a dissatisfied customer, vendor or other person. Take this as a sign you are doing something right — they are coming to you to solve a problem, rather than complaining to other potential customers. You need to relax; it isn't all about you, and everyone deals with dissatisfied customers at one point or another. So like all successful companies, you need to have a 'plan' with regard to how you will deal with complaints. A good plan starts before a complaint is made by knowing your client's needs and expectations so you can be proactive in dealing with customers.

Next you need to be sure you understand what the complaint actually is. Frankly, many complaints are the result of mere misunderstandings, so be sure you understand what the person is actually coming to you about. Be on the lookout for any underlying issues beyond the surface, but be prepared to also accept the complaint as valid and investigate it thoroughly. Tell them you appreciate this opportunity to improve your business, and that you are grateful they trusted you enough to approach you with this problem. If you don't say exactly that, at least think it and display this attitude. Treat it as a free learning opportunity for you.

If the complaint is about one of your employees, do not blindly sell out your employee in hopes it will keep the client/customer. If the complaint is groundless you risk losing a good employee, isolating the rest of your staff and also a customer, who will secretly see you as weak or doubt your judgment. Assure your client that you are going to investigate it thoroughly, then do so. Try to find a resolution which provides a win-win scenario. Perhaps your employees need to learn some new skills, and you can honestly assure the client that you learned something new.

Whatever the situation may be, clients need to know and believe that their complaint is listened to, understood and dealt with. The solution is figuring out what everyone requires to fulfill their needs. Sometimes even just listening well is a solution in itself. So try not to be on the defensive. Repeat what they've told you to make sure you've got it right. Ask them, if appropriate, what they feel might be an adequate solution. If the client is reasonable, your job is already done. If they're unreasonable, at least you know that right off the bat and know what their starting position is.

Remember: while you have the power as the provider, your client has the power in terms of future transactions, and their circle of influence. The ideal outcome means you both walk away satisfied with increased trust and goodwill and knowledge.

Complaints aren't just inconveniences — complaints can be useful tools for you to make your business better and more successful, and win a loyal customer (and all the people they recommend in future) for life.

Jeff Says: *Sometimes it's useful to try on another person's point of view just for a moment to get an idea of where they are coming from.*

"Good manners will open doors that the best education cannot."
—Clarence Thomas

Good Manners

Your mom was right: good manners matter, and make your day easier. Also, good manners are a key part of a successful business strategy, creating an attitude of respect, etiquette, politeness. Remember that all important first impression, and the Golden Rule to "do unto others as you would have them do unto you." What you send out comes back to roost.

Smile, make eye contact, give that person your attention -- all of your attention. Turn off your blackberry/cell phone if you are in a meeting, and do the same when you're on the phone. Find a private place that is distraction-free so that you can focus on them and take notes related to the task at hand. Use your customer's name, and if you aren't sure you are pronouncing the person's name correctly, ask them. If it is a name difficult to pronounce, that person likely would be thankful for having someone caring and respectful enough to ask. If you are phoning them, ask if you have caught them at a good time, and if it isn't, when would be more convenient? You are showing consideration for other people in these simple common-sense ways.

A positive attitude is much more attractive to someone than cynicism or negativity. People know that how you talk about others is how you will talk about them. People do business with people they trust. Good manners show your business to be trustworthy and a good positive attitude shows that you will be pleasant to deal with, even if the going gets tough.

Good manners with customers follow naturally from good manners in your office and workplace (and home). By modeling good manners you will see less disparaging, negative and sarcastic comments being thrown around your office. Your employees will feel valued and appreciated and look forward to coming to work, rather than feeling like their paycheque isn't enough reason to merit living in a war zone.

Be sure to say 'thank you' to employees, vendors and those who do a good job or go that little extra kilometer for your business. Thank your customers for their business. Remember, customers have other choices. When they choose you, good manners will reinforce the fact they've made a good decision.

Scott Says: *I always give people the benefit of the doubt until I am proved wrong otherwise. Be sure to make policies in your office to treat every customer the same. Those same policies can protect you from not getting paid. Many times I get repeat work just because I treat people with the utmost respect and professionalism.*

"Make your top managers rich and they will make you rich" **—Robert H. Johnson**

Hiring Family

Is it a good idea, or a bad one? Hiring family can be a good idea in some situations — if you're working with sensitive information, or you need someone you can trust. With family, you generally know what you're getting; there's no need to check the references, and you may share similar values and approaches.

It is especially meaningful to create employment for family members and loved ones — another way of taking care of people important to you — and may lead to increased job satisfaction for everyone. Getting family involved, especially immediate family, will include them in your successes (and failures) and give them a stake in your business.

Working with spouses can allow a couple to spend time together, improve communications, and work towards mutual goals. If you're raising kids, it can mean the kids are able to stay home longer which is beneficial to both the children and the family unit while reducing child care costs.

But, working with family doesn't have to mean everyone with your last name is on your payroll. It can be as simple as getting occasional feedback on your work, services, product, or presentation. Family members can test things you create. And you can arrange one-time contracts, or odd jobs here and there, as the opportunity presents itself and they are available.

Of course, there are also times when working with family is a bad idea. You want to avoid nepotism, or the appearance of nepotism, at all costs — the practice of hiring someone only because they're family, without consideration of their skills is counter to sound business practice and shouldn't be your sole criteria, particularly in key positions.

Another consideration is that when the work arrangement comes to an end — especially an unexpected end — it may disrupt family unity and create hard feelings. There may be situations, particularly dysfunctional ones, where it might not be the best idea to work together. Use good judgment.

If you do hire family, make sure you set the expectations up front in terms of what you want, and the likely length of the position. Put everything in writing, and further discuss the situation to be sure it is clear to everyone. Job descriptions, expectations, hours, wages, the length of the contract — everything you can think of should be detailed in writing and spelled out as clearly as possible. This is of prime importance with family. If disagreements arise, go immediately to the written description/contract for resolution so that the situation doesn't become emotional, destructive, or a source for bad feelings.

After all, no business is worth losing your entire family for! You are building a business so you can provide for your family — not eliminate them from your life.

Scott Says: *Some of my best and worst experiences in my self-employment have been when I hired family. Writing this book with my brother was a great decision because he has better project management than I do and we have the same motivation to get things done.*

About The Authors

Scott and Jeff Ward are two innovative young Aboriginal entrepreneurs based on Vancouver Island. Learn more about these two brothers at http://www.wardboys.biz

Scott Ward is a highly sought-after First Nation/Aboriginal stage hypnotist, performing comedy hypnosis shows for all ages and audiences. Scott holds a Bachelor of Education from the University of Alberta and is also certified in hypnotherapy.

In 2007 Scott was awarded an Alberta Business Award of Distinction from the Alberta Chamber of Commerce for his business success among other numerous community volunteer and service awards. Scott also worked previously as a career counselor and teacher before taking his comedy hypnosis shows on the road full-time in 2004.

Website: http://www.hypnotistscottward.com
Twitter: @hypnochief

Jeff Ward is a professional web creative, entrepreneur and proud father. In 2003, Jeff founded Animikii Inc., a web-services company building web-applications and online user experiences for community-based organizations across North America.

While in high school, Jeff was hired by an online education company as a web design consultant, inspiring the creation of his first company at the age of 17. He then went to specialize in user interface design with several start-up companies in California's Silicon Valley.

In 2009 Jeff was recognized as a role model by the National Aboriginal Health Organization. In 2010 Jeff was awarded the "Entrepreneur of The Year" title by the BC Achievement Foundation.

Website: http://jeff.io
Twitter: @jeffio

Andréa Ledding is an award-winning freelance journalist, writer, poet, and editor based in Saskatchewan, and was integral in helping put this book together.